Adventures in Scripture for Kids: Exploring The Full Armor of God

Lorie Eubank

GTO Publishing Solutions, LLC.

Contents

Introduction: "Armor Up!": Discovering God's Protection

Hello, young champions of faith! We're about to embark on an incredible journey that will lead us through the pages of the Bible to discover the amazing Armor of God. This isn't just any armor; it's a special set of tools that God gives us to stay strong and courageous in our daily lives.

The significance of the Armor of God:

Imagine wearing a belt of truth that helps you tell right from wrong or carrying a shield of faith that can protect you from fears and doubts. These aren't just pieces of metal and leather; they're symbols of God's love and strength that are always with us, even though we can't see them with our natural eyes.

In our expedition through the Scriptures, we'll engage in a remarkable exploration of the Armor of God. Each piece of the armor represents a core principle that empowers us to live as God intends, strong and full of hope. Let's put on the shoes of peace!

As we walk the paths of our daily lives, these shoes remind us to step gently and peacefully, spreading kindness and the good news that God loves us and wants us to live in peace with one another. Next, let's envision fastening the belt of truth around our waists. This isn't any ordinary belt; it's the foundation that holds everything together. Just as a belt secures the clothes of a warrior, truth secures our spiritual lives, ensuring the snares of deception do not trip us up.

Then, we have the breastplate of righteousness guarding our hearts. Righteousness, my young friends, is about being right with God—living in a way that pleases Him. This breastplate defends us against the wrongs that try to pierce our hearts, teaching us to choose actions that shine with God's goodness.

The helmet of salvation is crucial, too. It's not just a piece of headgear but a symbol of what Jesus has done for us. By accepting God's salvation through Jesus, we protect our minds from thoughts that can lead us astray. It's like having an invisible helmet that whispers, "You are loved and saved."

The sword of the Spirit, God's word, is unique. It's not for hurting but for healing, defeating the principalities of darkness by using the Word of God, and triumphing over temptation. Knowing and speaking God's word can cut through confusion and stand firm in truth.

Lastly, the shield of faith—what a wondrous defense it is! Our faith in God's promises can extinguish the flaming arrows of fear, worry, and doubt. Nothing can shake us when we lift our shields high, believing in God's power and love.

These symbols are powerful reminders of God's love and strength, ever-present, guiding, and protecting us in a world that often feels like a battleground. Remember, dear ones, our physical eyes do not see the Armor of God, but it is felt and witnessed in our actions, choices, and the unwavering spirit within us. As we journey together, we'll learn to wear this armor not just in our imaginations but in our everyday lives.

You might ask, "How can this armor help me today?" That's a fantastic question! Together, we will learn how the truth can defend us against lies, how righteousness can keep our hearts right, and how the good news of peace can guide our steps. We will see how faith can block out worries, how salvation keeps our thoughts safe, and how God's word is better than any sword in battle. This armor is real and powerful, and God gives it to us to use every single day.

Laying the foundation for the adventures ahead:
As we dive into the Bible and the stories of God's people, we'll see how they used this armor in their lives. And just like them, we can use it too! You'll learn how to put on each piece of God's Armor through thoughtful questions and exciting stories. So, let's open our hearts and minds as we step into the Bible's truths, ready to "Armor Up!" and learn how to stand strong in God's

mighty power. It's time to explore one of the greatest adventures of all, walking in the full Armor of God every day!

Chapter 1: The Shoes of Peace

Stepping Out in Faith

When we talk about stepping out in faith while wearing the Shoes of Peace, we are discussing a very special kind of trust in God. Imagine you're getting ready for a big adventure, but instead of packing a bag, you slip on the shoes God gave you. These aren't ordinary shoes; they carry you forward, even when you're unsure of the path ahead. Just as the Lord said to Joshua, "I will be with you; I will never leave you nor forsake you" (Joshua 1:5, NIV), we know that wearing these shoes means God is with us on our journey.

Understanding that we have the peace of God with us gives us the courage to take steps we might otherwise be too scared to take. Remember David, the young shepherd who faced Goliath?

He didn't wear the king's armor; he stepped out with just a sling and his faith in God (1 Samuel 17:38-50). His trust wasn't in protective gear or even in his strength—it was in the Lord's power. So when we wear our Shoes of Peace, we can step out in faith, knowing that God's peace is a sign that He is with us, guiding our steps.

Understanding the Gospel of Peace

The "gospel of peace" sounds like a beautiful phrase, but what does it mean? The word "gospel" means good news, and this good news is about peace—peace between us and God and peace between each other. This is the message that Jesus brought to Earth, which heals and brings together, like in Ephesians 2:14, where Jesus is called "our peace," the one who breaks down the walls that separate us.

Wearing the Shoes of Peace means we understand this message deeply and want to live it out. It's like walking a path that has been smoothed out by Jesus' love and sacrifice, making it possible for us to go and share this peace with others. When Jesus sent out His disciples, He told them, "Peace be with you! As the Father has sent me, I am sending you" (John 20:21, NIV). He was giving them—and us—the mission to walk in His peace and spread it everywhere we go.

Importance of Being Prepared and Ready

Just like a scout packs their bag with the essentials before a hike, we must be prepared for the journey God calls us on. The Shoes of Peace are part of that preparation. They remind us to be ready to move when God says it's time—being prepared means knowing the good news of Jesus so well that it's like a song in our hearts, ready to be sung at any moment.

The apostle Peter tells us, "Always be prepared to give an answer to everyone who asks you to give the reason for the hope that you have" (1 Peter 3:15, NIV). This doesn't mean we need to have all the answers, but we should be ready to share the love and peace of Jesus with anyone we meet. The Shoes of Peace help us to stand firm in what we believe and to walk confidently, sharing God's word just as the disciples did on their many travels, bringing the message of peace to new places and new faces.

Biblical Instances of Those Ready to Share God's Word

Throughout the Bible, there are many examples of individuals who were ready and eager to share God's word. Take Philip, for example. In Acts 8:26-40, the Spirit told Philip to go to a desert road, where he met an Ethiopian official reading about the prophet Isaiah. Philip ran up to his chariot and was ready to explain the scriptures, leading the official to faith in Jesus. Philip was prepared, with his Shoes of Peace on, ready to walk wherever God led him to spread the good news.

Another example is the apostle Paul. In Acts 16:9-10, Paul had a vision of a man in Macedonia begging him, "Come over to Macedonia and help us." After the vision, Paul and his companions got ready to leave for Macedonia, concluding that God had called them to preach the gospel to them. They were always prepared to share the word of God, understanding that the Shoes of Peace are not just for standing but for going out into the world to spread the peace of Christ.

Adventures of Evangelism

Evangelism is a big word that means telling others the good news about Jesus. It's a bit like being a messenger in a royal court, sent out with an important announcement for the entire kingdom. But instead of a king or queen sending us, it's God who gives us the message, and our kingdom is the whole wide world!

Jonah is sent to Nineveh

When we think of someone sent on an adventure to share God's message, we can't forget Jonah. God told him to go to Nineveh, a big city with many people who were not living the way God wanted them to. At first, Jonah was scared and ran away! But

God showed him that when He sends us on a mission, it's important to listen because He has a plan. After spending three days in the belly of a big fish, Jonah went to Nineveh and told the people what God wanted him to say. And guess what? They listened! They changed their ways, and God had mercy on them (see the Book of Jonah). Jonah's story teaches us that even when we're scared to share God's word, He is with us, and He can do amazing things through us when we listen to Him.

Spreading the Word in Our Communities

You don't have to be a grown-up to spread God's word; you can do it right where you are, in your own community! Just like Jesus' disciples walked around telling people about Jesus, we can share His love with our friends, our family, and even with people we meet while playing at the park or during a day at school. It can be as simple as being kind to someone who is sad, talking about why you love going to church, or even inviting a friend to come to Sunday school with you.

Activities and Reflections

Engaging in activities and reflections can help you better understand how to live out your faith and share God's love with others.

Let's explore some ways you can do this, whether on your own, with friends, or with your family.

Map: Planning Your Journey of Sharing

Create a map of your world—it can be a drawing of your neighborhood, school, or anywhere you spend time. On this map, mark places where you can share God's love. Maybe it's a friend's house, the local park, or a family member's kitchen table. Next to each place, write down how you might share God's love there. Will you tell a friend about Jesus? Will you show kindness to a new kid at school? This map will help you plan your journey of sharing the good news.

As you look at your map, think about Jesus' Great Commission: "Go therefore and make disciples of all nations" (Matthew 28:19). Although you might not be traveling to distant countries, your community is a great place to start fulfilling this mission!

Team Challenge: Sharing God's Love in Fun Ways

Form a team with your friends, Sunday school class, or family, and come up with creative ways to share God's love. Maybe you'll organize a community cleanup, make cards for people in a nursing home, or put on a play about a Bible story for your neighbors. Each act of kindness is a way to share God's love.

After completing each activity, gather your team to talk about the experience. What did you learn? How did it feel to work together and share God's love? Reflect on Galatians 5:13, which says, "Serve one another humbly in love." Each time you serve others, you are sharing God's love.

Family Discussion: Being Ambassadors of Peace

As a family, you can discuss what it means to be ambassadors of peace. An ambassador is someone who represents a country or a leader. Just like ambassadors, we are called to represent Jesus wherever we go. Read 2 Corinthians 5:20, which talks about being Christ's ambassadors, and discuss what this looks like in your family's daily life.

Questions for your family discussion might include: How can we show God's peace at home, at work, at school, or with our friends? Can you think of a time when you made peace in a difficult situation? What can we do to better represent Jesus to those around us?

These activities and reflections can help you put your faith into action and share Jesus's peace in practical, tangible ways. Remember, even the smallest pebble creates ripples in the water—so, too, your actions and words can have a big impact in sharing God's love and peace.

As we tie the laces of our Shoes of Peace, ready to step out and spread harmony wherever we go, let's remember that our journey with God is both sure-footed and purposeful. Now, with our feet firmly grounded in His peace, let's gird ourselves with the Belt of Truth, preparing our hearts and minds to embrace and live out the ultimate truth found in God's Word. Onward we march, from walking in peace to standing strong in truth!

Chapter 2: The Belt of Truth

"And you know the truth, and the truth will set you free."
John 8:32

Securing our Foundations

The Belt of Truth is like the part of our spiritual armor that holds everything else in place. In ancient times, soldiers would wear a belt around their waist to keep their armor secure and carry their weapons. It was essential for being ready for battle. In the same way, the Bible teaches us that truth is the foundation for everything we do as followers of Jesus. Ephesians 6:14 says, "Stand firm then, with the belt of truth buckled around your waist," which tells us that truth is what holds us up and keeps us ready for whatever comes our way.

Having the Belt of Truth means we are secure in knowing who God is, who we are in Him, and what He promises us in His Word. It's the truth of the Bible that keeps us from believing lies and getting confused. Jesus said in John 17:17, "Sanctify them by the truth; your word is truth." This means that God's Word makes us pure and sets us apart for Him, and it's the truth that makes us different from the world. When we know God's truth, we can stand firm like a house built on solid rock, not shifting with the winds or washing away with the rain (Matthew 7:24-25).

Understanding the Meaning of Truth

Truth isn't just about facts; it's about being real and reliable. It's something that stays the same, no matter what else changes. For Christians, the meaning of truth starts with God because He is the source of all truth. The Bible says in John 14:6 that Jesus declared, "I am the way and the truth and the life." This means that everything about Jesus—His life, His words, His love—is the truth we can always trust.

Putting on the Belt of Truth means we try to live like Jesus, who was always true in what He said and did. We use the Bible as our guidebook for truth, helping us understand right from wrong. When we tell the truth and live by it, we reflect Jesus' character to the world. It's like a bright light that guides us and shows others the way (Psalm 119:105). In a world that sometimes doesn't value truth, choosing to be truthful is a powerful way to show we belong to Jesus.

The Significance of Honesty in Our Daily Life

Being honest in our daily lives is like walking in bright daylight where everyone can see clearly. It builds trust and shows that we are followers of Jesus, who is the truth. When we tell the truth, we don't have to remember what we said to whom; we can be at peace, knowing that our words match our actions. Colossians 3:9-10 (NLT) tells us, "Do not lie to each other, for you have stripped off your old sinful nature and all it's wicked deeds. Put on your new nature, and be renewed as you learn to know your Creator and become like Him." This means that being honest is part of becoming more like God, who made us.

Honesty is not just about not telling lies; it's also about living in a way that's true to God's teachings. When we make good and right choices, even when it's hard or when no one else is looking, we are wearing our Belt of Truth tightly. These daily choices build a life of honesty and integrity, which is like a shining light that guides us and those around us to God (Proverbs 12:22).

Bible Stories Exemplifying Truthfulness

There are many stories in the Bible about people who chose to be truthful. One such person was Nathanael. When Jesus saw Nathanael approaching, He said, "Here truly is an Israelite in whom there is no deceit" (John 1:47, NIV). Jesus praised

Nathanael for being honest and truthful, without trickery or lies.

Another example of truthfulness is the story of Queen Esther. She revealed her true identity and stood up for her people, even though it was risky. Her honesty and bravery saved her people from great danger (Book of Esther). By telling the truth, Esther showed great faith and courage. These stories encourage us to wear our Belt of Truth proudly and to be honest like Nathanael and brave like Esther, knowing that God values and works through those who live in truth.

Adventures of Honesty

Honesty is like a bright light that guides us through the dark, showing us the way and keeping us safe from stumbling. When we wear the Belt of Truth, we wrap ourselves in this light, ensuring that every step we take aligns with God's truth. But what happens when we choose to ignore this vital piece of armor?

Story of Ananias and Sapphira

In the Book of Acts, we find a cautionary tale about Ananias and Sapphira, a husband and wife who decided to be dishonest with their community and, more importantly, with God. They sold a piece of property and, wanting to appear more generous than they were, they lied about the amount of money they received, keeping part of it for themselves. They thought they could deceive the apostles and the early Christian community, but God saw their hearts.

Peter confronted Ananias, asking, "Ananias, how is it that Satan has so filled your heart that you have lied to the Holy Spirit and have kept for yourself some of the money you received for the land?" (Acts 5:3, NIV). When Ananias heard this, he fell down and died, and the same fate met Sapphira when she also lied. This shocking event was a powerful reminder to the early church of the seriousness of honesty and the consequences of deceit.

Consequences of Not Wearing the Belt of Truth

Ananias and Sapphira's story isn't just a tale from long ago; it's a lesson for us about the importance of truth in our lives. When we choose not to wear the Belt of Truth, we open ourselves up to small compromises that can lead to big consequences. Just like a tiny crack in a dam can eventually cause it to break, a small lie can lead to more dishonesty, hurting us and those around us.

Not wearing the Belt of Truth can also separate us from God. God is truth, and when we live in dishonesty, we move away from Him. Like Ananias and Sapphira, we might think we're only deceiving people, but in reality, we're also trying to hide from God, which is impossible. Psalm 51:6 says, "Yet you desired faithfulness even in the womb; you taught me wisdom in that secret place." This verse reminds us that God values truth deep within us, in the secret places of our hearts where only He can see.

Wearing the Belt of Truth isn't always easy, but the story of Ananias and Sapphira teaches us that honesty is not optional for those who follow Christ. It's a crucial part of our armor, protecting us from the inside out and keeping us close to God, who is the source of all truth.

Activities and Reflections

Integrating the Belt of Truth into our daily lives can be enlightening and fun. Through activities like games, journaling, and family discussions, we can explore the value of honesty in a tangible and memorable way. Ephesians 4:25 urges, "Therefore each of you must put off falsehood and speak truthfully to your neighbor, for we are all members of one body."

Journaling: A Day of Complete Honesty

Encourage yourself and a friend to keep a journal for a day, recording every time they are faced with a choice, to be honest or not. At the end of the day, reflect on how being honest made them feel, what challenges they faced, and what they learned about the value of truth.

This reflective practice can help deepen our understanding of Proverbs 12:22, which says, "The Lord detests lying lips, but he delights in people who are trustworthy." Journaling about our experiences with honesty can help us see more clearly how truth impacts our relationship with God and others, and how, like the Belt of Truth, it holds together the integrity of our character.

Family Discussion: The Importance of Truth at Home

Set aside time for a family discussion about the importance of truth in your household. Talk about why being honest is crucial and how it affects the trust and respect between family members. You can share stories from the Bible, like the story of Ananias and Sapphira, to illustrate the consequences of dishonesty and the blessings of living truthfully.

This conversation can be anchored in scriptures like Zechariah 8:16, which advises, "Speak the truth to each other, and render true and sound judgment in your courts." Discussing the role of truth at home reinforces the idea that honesty strengthens the family unit, builds trust, and creates a safe space where every member feels valued and understood. It's a practical way to weave the Belt of Truth into the fabric of everyday life, ensuring that the principles of God's Word are lived out not just in words but in actions and interactions within the home.

Chapter 3: The Breastplate of Righteousness

"I walk in righteousness, in paths of justice." Proverbs 8:20

Welcome to another chapter in our Adventures in Scriptures! We're diving into an essential piece of the Armor of God: the Breastplate of Righteousness. Just like a knight wears a breastplate to protect his heart in battle, God gives us righteousness to guard our hearts from things that might try to hurt us.

Protecting the Heart -What Righteousness Means

Righteousness is indeed a big word with an even bigger meaning, especially when we think about how it fits into our lives as followers of Jesus. You see, righteousness is all about living in a way that is right and good, just like you learned. But here's an amazing secret: the righteousness we wear as part of our spiritual armor doesn't actually come from the good things we do. It comes from Jesus Christ Himself!

When Jesus came to Earth, lived a perfect life, and chose to die on the cross for us, He did something extraordinary. He took all the wrong things we've ever done or will do and said, "I've got this. I'll take your sin on Me." And in exchange, He gives us His righteousness. It's like if you had a really messy, scribbled-on piece of paper and Jesus said, "Here, take My clean, perfect piece of paper instead." 2 Corinthians 5:21 explains this beautifully: "God made him who had no sin to be sin for us, so that in him we might become the righteousness of God."

This means that when God looks at us, He doesn't see our mistakes or the times we haven't been perfect. Instead, He sees us as right and good because He sees Jesus' goodness covering us. This is why we can wear the Breastplate of Righteousness and protect our hearts. It's not about being perfect on our own; it's about trusting that Jesus has made us right with God.

Knowing that our righteousness comes from Jesus helps us make choices that please God and show love and respect to others. We do this not because we're trying to earn God's love but because we're so grateful for what Jesus has done for us. It's like wearing a thank-you note close to our hearts, reminding us to live in a way that honors Him. So, when you think about righteousness, remember it's a gift from Jesus. We wear it to protect our hearts, to remind us of His love, and to help us live in a way that reflects His goodness and love to the world around us.

Why Our Heart Needs Protection

Our heart is like a treasure chest that holds everything we care about the most. It's where our feelings, like love and joy, come from, but it's also where we feel sadness and fear. Just like a treasure chest must be kept safe from pirates, our hearts need protection from things that could hurt or lead us astray.

Sometimes, we might see something we want, even if it's not good for us, like maybe taking a toy that isn't ours or saying something unkind to get a laugh from others. These moments are like tests, challenging what's in our hearts and what we truly believe is important. The Breastplate of Righteousness, given to us by God, acts like a strong, shiny armor over our treasure chest, helping us remember what's truly valuable—being kind, honest, and loving like Jesus.

This breastplate doesn't just keep the bad stuff out; it also keeps the good things in, like peace, joy, and love. When we choose to follow Jesus and let His righteousness protect us, our hearts become like well-guarded treasure chests full of God's goodness. This means even when things get tough or we're tempted to make wrong choices, we can remember the love of Jesus that guards our hearts and choose to do what's right.

Biblical Figures Who Wore Their Breastplate Well

Many people in the Bible showed us how to wear the Breastplate of Righteousness.

Daniel in the Lion's Den

Daniel is a shining example of someone who wore his Breastplate of Righteousness exceptionally well. In the face of laws that forbade praying to anyone other than the king, Daniel continued to pray to God, not hiding his faith even when it meant facing deadly consequences. His commitment to righteousness and his unwavering faith in God protected him when he was thrown into a den of lions, a situation where any physical armor would have been useless. God sent an angel to shut the lions' mouths, and Daniel emerged unharmed, demonstrating the protective power of spiritual integrity (Daniel 6).

Esther's Courage and Wisdom

Esther, a young Jewish girl who became queen, also displayed remarkable righteousness. When her people were threatened with being destroyed, Esther had to make a choice. She could stay silent and protect herself or risk her life to save her people. Esther chose righteousness, fasting, praying, and then bravely approaching the king to plead for her people. Her righteous actions, guided by faith and love, led to the salvation of the Jews in Persia (Esther 4-8).

Job's Enduring Faith

Job's story is a powerful testament to the strength of the Breastplate of Righteousness in withstanding personal loss and suffering. Despite losing everything he held dear, Job refused to curse God or turn away from his righteousness. His faith was tested through extreme trials, yet he maintained his integrity, not understanding why he suffered but refusing to compromise his righteousness before God. In the end, God restored Job's fortunes, doubling what he had lost, and blessed his latter days more than his beginning (Job 1-42).

Mary's Humble Submission

Mary, the mother of Jesus, exemplified righteousness through her humble obedience and faith. When told by the angel Gabriel that she would conceive the Son of God, Mary responded with faith, despite the potential for social scorn and misunderstanding. Her response, "I am the Lord's servant, may everything you have said about me come true." reflects a heart fully committed to God's will, protected by righteousness even in the face of uncertainty and potential danger (Luke 1:26-38).

Righteousness, like a sturdy breastplate, keeps us safe when we're faced with choices. Daniel could have decided not to pray and avoid trouble, but his commitment to doing right kept him safe, even in a den of hungry lions. It shows us that when we're faced with tough decisions, choosing what's right according to God's way can protect us from harm.

Activities and Reflections – Craft: Design Your Breastplate

Grab some craft supplies, and let's make our own breastplates! You can use cardboard as the base and decorate it with symbols that represent righteousness to you. It could be a heart to show love, a cross to remind us of Jesus, or anything that helps you remember to choose what's right.

Role-playing: Tough Choices Scenarios

Act out different scenarios with your friends or family where you have to make a tough choice. Maybe you find money and have to decide whether to keep it or find the owner, or someone asks you to cheat on a test. Discuss what the righteous choice would be in each situation.

Family Discussion: Daily Acts of Righteousness

Gather your family and talk about small ways to practice righteousness daily. It could be sharing with a sibling, doing your chores without being asked, or standing up for someone who's being treated unfairly. Together, you can make a plan to help each other remember and choose righteousness every day.

Remember, our righteousness comes from Jesus as a gift. Wearing the Breastplate of Righteousness is about making choices that protect our hearts and show love to God and others. Just like Daniel and many others in the Bible, we can face any challenge bravely when we choose what's right. Remember, righteousness isn't just for the big moments; it's for every choice we make, big or small. So, let's put on our breastplates and set out on today's adventure, ready to do what's right!

Chapter 4: The Helmet of Salvation

"Restore to me the joy of your salvation, and make me willing to obey you." Psalm 51:12

Just as a helmet protects a soldier's head in battle, the Helmet of Salvation guards our minds, keeping our thoughts focused on God's great love and the salvation He offers us through Jesus. If you look at the picture on the cover, you will notice that the helmet covers the head, including the ears and mouth. You need the guard over your ears and mouth to protect the gates to your heart. When we give our hearts to God and accept Jesus as Our Savior, He lives in our hearts. It changes you from the inside out. Having Jesus in your heart makes you change your words; you want to be kinder to others. You want to listen to different and better things that encourage and lift you up. It changes the way you think and feel about things.

Guarding the Mind – Understanding Salvation's Significance

Salvation is a beautiful gift from God. Jesus was on a rescue mission, not to judge mankind but to save us from sin and its consequences. By believing in Jesus and what He did for us on the cross, we are saved and become part of God's family forever. This amazing truth is something we keep in our minds, just like wearing a helmet on our heads. When our enemy Satan comes to tell us we are in trouble with God or that God is mad at us, we can remember that if we repent, God will forgive us. Through forgiveness, we are restored to God's family.

How Our Thoughts Guide Our Actions

What we think about really matters because our thoughts often turn into actions. If we fill our minds with the truth about God's love and salvation, we're more likely to live in a way that shows we belong to Jesus. The Bible says in Philippians 4:8 to think about things that are true, noble, right, pure, lovely, and admirable. Keeping our minds on these things is like keeping our helmets strapped on tight. When we spend time reading our Bibles, we learn what good and pleasing behavior is in the eyes of God. As we think about these things, they become our actions, and people watching us can see how salvation through Jesus has changed us from the inside out.

In 2 Corinthians 3:2, "You yourselves are our letter, written on our hearts, known and read by everyone." People watch and see how your heart and mind have changed, followed by how you behave and the powerful impact Jesus has made in your life. You probably feel pretty powerful when you consider the other armor you are also wearing, the Shoes of Peace, the Belt of Truth, and the Breastplate of Righteousness.

Bible Heroes Who Remained Mentally Strong

Paul and Silas kept their minds focused on God, even when things got tough. Think about when they were thrown into prison for telling people about Jesus. Even there, they prayed and sang hymns to God (Acts 16:25). Their minds were guarded by the Helmet of Salvation, keeping them strong in faith despite their circumstances.

Paul and Silas are not the only Bible heroes who demonstrated incredible mental strength and resilience, safeguarded by what we can liken to the Helmet of Salvation. Their ability to maintain focus on God and express joy through singing and prayer, even in dire circumstances, is a powerful testament to the strength that comes from a deep-rooted faith in God. This same kind of mental fortitude, anchored in faith, is evident in the lives of several other biblical figures.

David's Confidence in God

David, before he became king, faced numerous life-threatening challenges that tested not only his physical strength but also his mental and emotional resilience. Facing Goliath, a giant warrior, David's confidence wasn't in his strength but in the power of God, who had delivered him from the paw of the lion and the bear. This trust in God's deliverance was David's mental armor, enabling him to confront and defeat Goliath against all odds (1 Samuel 17). Throughout his life, despite various trials, including being pursued by King Saul, David continually sought God's guidance. He expressed his fears, hopes, and gratitude through the Psalms, demonstrating his mental strength rooted in his relationship with God.

Elijah's Recovery and Renewal

After a significant victory on Mount Carmel, where he triumphed over the prophets of Baal, Elijah found himself fleeing for his life from Queen Jezebel's threats. In a moment of fear and exhaustion, he prayed for death. However, God met Elijah in his despair, providing food, rest, and a gentle whisper to strengthen and reassure him. This encounter shows the importance of spiritual and mental restoration, where God's gentle presence and provision can renew our minds and spirits, helping us to stand firm again (1 Kings 19).

Jesus in the Wilderness

Jesus Himself, after being baptized, faced a significant mental and spiritual test in the wilderness for forty days. During this time, He was tempted by Satan but countered every temptation with Scripture, demonstrating the power of God's Word to protect and strengthen the mind. Jesus' use of Scripture as a defense showcases the ultimate example of the Helmet of Salvation and the Sword of the Spirit at work, ensuring mental and spiritual integrity in the face of temptation (Matthew 4:1-11).

These stories illustrate that mental strength in the face of trials, rooted in faith, is a key aspect of spiritual resilience. Just as Paul and Silas worshipped in prison, Job held onto his integrity, David trusted in God's deliverance, God's gentle care restored Elijah, and Jesus wielded the Word of God in the wilderness, we too are called to guard our minds with the truth and hope of salvation, standing firm in our faith no matter the circumstances.

Adventures of Redemption

The story of Paul, formerly known as Saul, is a powerful testament to the transformative power of the Helmet of Salvation. Initially, Saul was a fervent persecutor of Christians, dedicated to eradicating the followers of Jesus. However, on his way to Damascus, a blinding light from heaven and the voice of Jesus stopped him in his tracks, leading to a profound personal transformation. Blinded and humbled, Saul was led into Damascus, where Ananias, a disciple of Jesus, healed him in the name of the Lord. This moment marked Saul's conversion, and he was baptized as Paul, dedicating his life to spreading the gospel of Christ. Paul's story, found in Acts 9:1-19, illustrates how the truth of salvation can dramatically change one's life and set them on a new path of righteousness and service to God.

Modern-day Distractions from Our Salvation

In the hustle and bustle of our modern lives, distractions are everywhere, vying for our attention and often pulling our focus away from the things that truly matter. For young minds especially, the allure of video games, the endless scroll of social media, and the constant bombardment of entertainment can make it challenging to keep our thoughts centered on Jesus and the incredible gift of salvation He offers.

The Allure of the Screen

Video games and social media aren't inherently bad. Still, they can become significant distractions when they consume too much of our time and energy—time and energy that could be spent building our relationship with God. These platforms are designed to keep us engaged, often making us crave the next level in a game or the next batch of "likes" on a post. This continuous loop of instant gratification can shift our focus from the eternal joy found in Jesus to temporary pleasures.

The Noise of the World

Beyond screens, the world around us is full of noise that can drown out God's still, small voice. From peer pressure at school to the latest trends and gadgets, getting caught up in wanting to fit in and have the newest, coolest things is easy. This pursuit can lead us away from the contentment and peace that come from knowing we are saved and loved by God, no matter what we have or what others think of us.

The Busyness Trap

Today's fast-paced lifestyle can also be a distraction. Our schedules are packed between school, sports, hobbies, and social events. It's easy to think we're too busy for prayer, Bible reading, or just being still and knowing He is God. This busyness can make us feel like we're wearing our helmets backward, unable to see or remember the direction we should be going—toward God.

Keeping Our Helmets On

Remembering to keep our "helmets" on means making a conscious effort to focus on what truly matters. It means setting aside time each day to talk to God, read His Word, and reflect on His love and the salvation He's given us. It's about choosing activities and entertainment that uplift and strengthen our faith rather than pull us away from it.

We can also use the tools of our modern world for good, like listening to worship music, watching uplifting content, or using apps designed to help us learn more about the Bible and stay connected to our faith community. It's about finding balance and making sure our hearts and minds are centered on Jesus.

Staying Focused in a World of Distractions

Staying focused on our salvation in a world full of distractions isn't always easy, but it's possible with God's help. Just like a ship uses an anchor to stay in place amidst the waves, our faith in Jesus is the anchor for our souls, keeping us steady and secure. When we feel ourselves getting pulled away by the distractions of the world, we can pray, asking God to help us refocus and remember the incredible love and salvation He offers.

By wearing our spiritual armor daily, especially the Helmet of Salvation, we can navigate the distractions of modern life with wisdom and discernment, keeping our eyes fixed on Jesus, the author, and perfecter of our faith.

Young Testimonies: Coming to Christ

There are many stories of kids, just like you, who have found hope and joy in Jesus. These young testimonies remind us that no one is too young to experience God's love and start a new life with Him. Hearing how others came to Christ can encourage us to share our stories and help our friends understand God's amazing salvation.

Activities and Reflections

Quiz: Test Your Knowledge of Salvation

Take a fun quiz with your friends or family to see what you know about salvation. Questions could include stories from the Bible, verses that discuss God's love and, Jesus' sacrifice, and what it means to be saved.

Crafting: Designing a Symbolic Helmet

Using paper, cardboard, or any other materials you like, craft a helmet that represents the salvation we have in Jesus. You can decorate it with symbols like crosses, hearts, or anything that reminds you of Jesus' love and the new life He gives us.

Family Discussion: Personal Salvation Stories

Gather with your family and share your own stories of how you came to understand what Jesus did for you. If some family members aren't sure yet, this can be a beautiful time to talk about any questions or thoughts they have about God and salvation. Sharing your personal journeys can help everyone see how real and life-changing God's love is.

The Helmet of Salvation is more than just a piece of armor; it's a constant reminder of our new life and our hope in Jesus. Keeping our minds focused on God's love helps us live out our salvation daily, showing the world the difference Jesus makes. So, let's put on our helmets, hold onto the truth of salvation, and step forward in faith, ready for whatever adventures God has in store for us!

Chapter 5: The Sword of the Spirit

For the word of God is living and powerful, and sharper than any two-edged sword, piercing even to the division of soul and spirit, and of joints and marrow, and is a discerner of the thoughts and intents of the heart. Hebrews 4:12

Next, we will explore a super cool piece of the Armor of God: The Sword of the Spirit. Imagine a sword that's not too heavy, not too light, and shines brighter than the sun. This isn't just any sword; it's special because it represents God's Word, the Bible!

Understanding the Bible's Power – Wielding God's Word

The Bible is like a treasure chest filled with amazing stories, powerful lessons, and God's promises to us. But it's not just a book to read at bedtime; it's like a sword that helps us in life. When we learn what the Bible says, we're like warriors learning how to use their swords. It helps us know right from wrong and teaches us about God's incredible love.

The Dual Nature of the Sword: Defense and Offense

Our Sword of the Spirit has two super important jobs. First, it's a weapon that protects us. When we remember Bible verses, we can use them to take captive bad thoughts or help us avoid wrong choices. Second, our sword can also be used like a scalpel, separating anything that is not of God from our lives. This would be like removing wrong thinking about different things. Things like selfishness, envy, unforgiveness, and so much more.

When you begin to know and walk in the word of God, you will feel a heaviness if you are carrying unforgiveness in your heart. In the Word, Jesus tells us to "forgive, and you will be forgiven" (Luke 6:37). You decide to forgive the person you held unforgiveness over, and suddenly, you feel free from that burden because you also know that God has forgiven you.

Bible Stories of the Word in Action

There are many wonderful Bible stories where God's Word is like a superhero's sword. Remember when Jesus was in the desert, and the sneaky devil tried to trick Him? Jesus used God's Word to stop the devil's tricks, saying, "It is written..." (Matthew 4:1-11). And then there's David, a young shepherd boy who defeated the giant Goliath not with a big sword but with his faith in God and a little sling (1 Samuel 17). These stories show us that knowing and believing God's Word gives us strength, just like a mighty sword. Besides Jesus in the desert and David facing Goliath, there are numerous other instances that highlight the Word in action.

Joshua and the Walls of Jericho

In the book of Joshua, we find the remarkable story of the walls of Jericho falling down. Joshua and the Israelites were facing a formidable obstacle: the massive walls of Jericho stood between them and the land God promised them. But God gave Joshua specific instructions, which might have seemed unusual at first. For six days, they were to march around the city once each day, and on the seventh day, they were to march around seven times; then, the priests would blow their trumpets, and everyone would shout. Joshua followed God's commands precisely, and on that seventh day, the walls of Jericho collapsed (Joshua 6). This story illustrates the power of obedience to God's Word and how faith in His instructions, no matter how unconventional they may seem, can lead to miraculous outcomes.

Elijah and the Prophets of Baal

The confrontation between Elijah and the prophets of Baal on Mount Carmel is another vivid example of God's Word in action. At a time when the Israelites were wavering between worshipping God and Baal, Elijah proposed a test to prove who the true God was. Each would prepare a bull as a sacrifice but not set fire to it; the god who answered by fire would be deemed the true God. Despite the prophets of Baal's loud cries and rituals, their god did not answer. But when Elijah prayed, God sent fire from heaven that consumed not only the sacrifice but even the stones and soil around it, and all the water in the trench Elijah had made. This powerful demonstration led the people to proclaim, "The Lord, He is God!" (1 Kings 18). Elijah's unwavering faith in God's promise and courage to stand alone against 450 prophets showcase the strength of adhering to God's Word.

Shadrach, Meshach, and Abednego

The story of Shadrach, Meshach, and Abednego in the fiery furnace is a stirring testament to the power of faith and God's Word. When King Nebuchadnezzar ordered everyone to worship a golden statue, these three young men refused, staying true to God's commandments. As a result, they were thrown into a blazing furnace, but their faith in God's protection was so strong that they were not harmed by the fire. In fact, a fourth figure, resembling a son of the gods, was seen walking with them in the furnace. Astonished, Nebuchadnezzar called them out, unharmed by the flames, and acknowledged the power of their God (Daniel 3). This story highlights how faith in God's Word can protect us in the face of life's fiercest trials.

The Centurion's Faith

In the New Testament, the story of the Roman centurion's faith in Jesus' authoritative word is a compelling example of belief in action. The centurion approached Jesus, asking Him to heal his servant. When Jesus offered to come to his house, the centurion expressed his unwavering faith in Jesus' spoken word alone, believing that if Jesus merely said the word, his servant would be healed. Marveling at such faith, Jesus declared it done, and the servant was healed at that very hour (Matthew 8:5-13). This account underscores the power inherent in Jesus' words and the miracles that faith in His word can bring about.

The Story of Nehemiah

In the bustling city of Jerusalem, a man named Nehemiah took on a great challenge. Jerusalem's walls were in ruins, leaving the city vulnerable. Nehemiah, guided by his faith and God's words, decided to rebuild these walls to protect his people. Despite facing many who wanted to stop him, Nehemiah used wisdom from God's word to stay strong and encourage his people. He prayed and kept God's promises close to his heart, which helped him complete the seemingly impossible task of rebuilding the walls of Jerusalem (Nehemiah 2-6). Nehemiah's story teaches us that we can face big challenges and make a difference with God's word in our hearts.

Each of these stories, from the fall of Jericho's walls to the unwavering faith of a Roman officer, teaches us about the extraordinary power of God's Word. Like a mighty sword, it has the power to break down barriers, protect us from harm, and heal the broken. As we learn and live by these words, we embark on a grand adventure, wielding the Sword of the Spirit to face challenges with courage, uphold truth, and spread God's love, just like the heroes of the Bible.

So, let's pick up our Sword of the Spirit and prepare for adventure! By learning and living by God's Word, we're not just reading stories; we're becoming part of the greatest adventure of all.

Challenges of Maintaining Spiritual Discipline

Staying disciplined in reading the Bible and praying every day can sometimes feel like a big task, especially when we'd rather play video games or watch TV. But just like a warrior practices with their sword every day to stay sharp, we need to keep our Sword of the Spirit sharp by reading God's Word and talking to Him in prayer. It might seem tough at first, but the more we do it, the stronger and wiser we'll become.

Kids Who Memorized and Used the Scripture

There are many stories of kids, just like you, who have memorized parts of the Bible and used them in amazing ways. Some kids have shared verses with friends who were sad or scared, and those words helped bring comfort and hope. Others have remembered verses when they felt afraid about courage, like "This is my command- Be strong and courageous! Do not be afraid or discouraged. For the Lord your God is with you wherever you go." (Joshua 1:9). By keeping God's Word in their hearts, these kids were able to spread light and love to those around them, showing the true power of the Sword of the Spirit.

Activities and Reflections

Memorize & Recite: A Verse a Day

Challenge yourself to learn a new Bible verse every day. You can write them on cards, draw pictures about them, or even make up a song. Start with verses about Courage, Love, Patience, Faith, and Hope. Share these verses with your family and friends, and encourage them to learn with you. By the end of the week, you'll have a collection of verses you know by heart, ready to use whenever you need them.

Family Discussion: The Bible's Role in Our Home

Gather your family and talk about how the Bible is like a treasure map for life. Discuss how everyone can help make sure that reading the Bible and praying together becomes a special part of your daily routine. Share your favorite Bible stories or verses and talk about how they have helped you or can help you in the future. This conversation will help make the Bible an important part of your family's adventure together.

We have learned that wielding the Sword of the Spirit is not just about knowing God's Word but living it out in our daily actions. By diving into stories of the past, practicing discipline, and sharing what we learn, we become true warriors of faith, ready to face the world with God's wisdom as our guide. So let's embark on this adventure with excitement, knowing that with our Sword of the Spirit in hand, we're never alone and always prepared.

Chapter 6: The Shield of Faith

As we continue learning about the Armor of God, we come to the final piece: The Shield of Faith. Imagine carrying a shield so strong that no matter what comes flying your way, you can stand safe and secure. This shield isn't made of wood or metal but of faith—your trust and belief in God's power and love.

Understanding Faith's Protective Role – Guarding Against Attacks

Faith is like an invisible shield that protects us. It's like holding up a shield in a battle when we believe in God and trust Him. This shield can stop all kinds of things that might try to hurt us, like fear, doubt, or feeling alone. It's not always easy to hold up our shield, especially when things get tough, but remembering God's promises helps keep our shield strong and in front of us.

The more we carry our shield, the stronger we get. The stronger we get carrying our shield, the bigger our shield becomes as our faith continues to grow.

Biblical Battles and the Power of Faith

The Bible is full of stories where faith acts as a powerful shield. Think about David, a young shepherd boy who faced a giant warrior named Goliath. David didn't wear heavy armor or carry a big sword as King Saul tried to have him do. No, he had faith in God and a simple slingshot. His trust and faith in God was his shield, and it was strong enough to defeat Goliath (1 Samuel 17). David's story teaches us that no matter how big our problems seem, our faith in God can help us overcome them.

Sometimes, we might feel doubt creeping into our thoughts, trying to make our shield of faith feel smaller and weaker. Maybe it's a scary situation or a time when a prayer feels unanswered. But remember Peter, who walked on water towards Jesus? When he kept his eyes on Jesus, he was walking just fine. But the moment he looked at the stormy waves and doubted, he began to sink (Matthew 14:29-31). Jesus helped him up, reminding him to keep his faith strong, no matter the storm.

Noah builds an Ark

Imagine being one of only a few people who believed it was important to follow God. And because you were the only one whom God found to be righteous in His sight, you were the one He chose to give a plan that would save your family and animals to one day replenish the earth. God chose Noah to offer the plans to build the ark. In obedience to God, he and his family would work building the ark for the next 100 years and making it ready. Now, you should know that before this time, they had not seen the rain; water came up from the ground to water the plants and provide water for the people.

Do you think people were making fun of Noah for building the ark in obedience to God? Because Noah was faithful to do all God instructed, when the great flood came, his family and all of the animals went into the ark, and the Lord closed the door. The storms and rains came, and all life was lost except Noah, his family, and the animals in the ark. This story shows us that our faith can do amazing things when we follow God's guidance, even when it's hard to understand.

Modern Challenges to Faith and Overcoming Them

Today, we might not face city walls like Jericho, but we will still face challenges. Maybe it's feeling left out at school, worrying about a test, or seeing bad things happen in the world. These situations can test our faith, but just like Joshua, we can remember God's promises and keep our Shield of Faith up. Talking to

God, reading the Bible, and sharing our feelings with family or friends can help make our shield even stronger.

Real-life Testimonies of Unyielding Faith

Many people, even kids, have amazing stories of how their faith helped them through tough times. These real-life testimonies inspire us and show that God is always with us, helping us hold our Shield of Faith high. Can you remember a time when you made a decision to do the right thing even when your friends were encouraging you to do something you might get in trouble for? Your faith shield got a little bigger when you chose to do the right thing. Remembering to do what is right in the eyes of the Lord, even when it is hard, shows your trust in the Lord to protect you and keep you safe.

Activities and Reflections

DIY: Crafting a Personal Shield

Let's get creative and make our own Shield of Faith! Use cardboard, paint, markers or crayons, and decorations to create a shield that represents your faith. You can draw symbols that remind you of God's love, strength, and promises. Whenever you see your shield, let it remind you of your faith in God.

Memory Verse Challenge: Strengthening Faith

Choose a Bible verse about faith that you love, and try to memorize it. You can write it down, make a drawing about it, or even set it to a tune to help you remember. This verse will be like a mini-shield you can carry in your heart, ready to use whenever you need a boost of faith.

Family Discussion: Remembering Moments of Faith

Gather with your family and share stories of times when your faith was like a shield for you. It could be a moment when you were scared but prayed and felt peace or when you trusted God with a big problem and saw Him help you through it. Sharing these moments can help everyone remember how powerful and important our faith is.

Holding up the Shield of Faith might take effort, especially when challenges come our way, but remember, with faith in God, we're never fighting alone. So, let's march forward with our shields held high, ready for whatever comes our way.

Chapter 7: Understanding the Real Battle

We have reviewed all of the different pieces of the Armor of God. Now, we will uncover the mysteries of the real battle we face every day. It's not like the battles you see in cartoons or video games; it's a special kind of fight that needs a special type of armor—the Armor of God!

Ephesians 6:12 Explained – Beyond Flesh and Blood

Ephesians 6:12 tells us that our real battle isn't against people we can see but against powerful forces in the spiritual world that we can't see with our eyes. These forces try to make us do wrong things or feel scared and alone, but God gives us special protection to stand strong against them.

The Spiritual Realm and Its Reality

Just like there's a world around us with trees, mountains, and oceans, there's also a spiritual world that we can't see. This world is filled with God's love and His angels, but also with principalities of spiritual darkness that bring challenges that we face in our hearts and minds. That's why we must put on the Armor of God to keep our hearts, minds, and spirits safe. In 2 Corinthians 10:4-5, Paul is telling the people, "We use God's mighty weapons, not worldly weapons, to knock down the strongholds of human reasoning and to destroy false arguments. We destroy every proud obstacle that keeps people from knowing God. We capture their rebellious thoughts and teach them to obey Christ."

The only way that Paul can do this is to know the word of God, to answer and proclaim the truth in the word, so that these people would be set free from their wrong thinking. Through prayer and taking authority over the lies of the enemy, they are able to reach the people with the word of God, setting them free from the spiritual enemy.

Bible Stories of Spiritual Warfare

There are many stories in the Bible where God's people faced big challenges with the help of God's strength. Remember David and Goliath? David didn't win because he was the biggest or the strongest; he won because he had faith in God's power to protect and help him (1 Samuel 17).

One of the Bible's foundational stories of spiritual warfare is the Exodus, where Moses leads the Israelites out of Egypt, away from Pharaoh's tyranny. The plagues that God sent upon Egypt, culminating in the Passover and the parting of the Red Sea, were not just physical manifestations of God's power but also acts of spiritual warfare against the gods of Egypt and the oppressive spirit of slavery. Moses' confrontations with Pharaoh and his reliance on God's instructions demonstrate a profound trust in God's sovereignty and power, highlighting the spiritual battle behind the physical liberation of the Israelites (Exodus 7-14).

The Apostle Paul's missionary journeys were fraught with both physical and spiritual opposition. In Ephesus, for example, Paul's preaching led to a significant decrease in the business of local silversmiths who made idols, causing a riot. This wasn't just a socio-economic conflict but a spiritual battle against the stronghold of idolatry in the city. Despite imprisonment, beatings, and shipwrecks, Paul's persistent ministry is a testimony of the ongoing spiritual warfare faced by those spreading the Gospel, emphasizing the victory that comes through perseverance and faith (Acts 19, 2 Corinthians 11:23-27).

Adventures Beyond Sight

The Armor of God in Action

The story of David and Goliath from 1 Samuel 17 is a compelling reflection of being ready for battle by embodying the principles of the whole armor of God. Although the story in the Bible doesn't directly mention the Armor of God as described in Ephesians 6, David's faith, actions, and words demonstrate what it means to be spiritually equipped for battle.

In this story, David, a young shepherd boy, faces Goliath, a giant warrior intimidating the armies of Israel. David's readiness for battle doesn't come from physical armor; in fact, he rejects King Saul's offer of traditional armor because it's cumbersome and unfamiliar to him. Instead, David goes into battle with a sling, five smooth stones, and, most importantly, an absolute faith in God.

David's trust in God as his protector and deliverer reflects the Shield of Faith, deflecting the figurative "fiery darts" of fear and doubt cast by Goliath's threats. His choice to face Goliath with just a sling and stones, relying on God's strength, mirrors the Sword of the Spirit, using God's word and promises as his offensive weapon. David declares to Goliath, "You come against me with sword and spear and javelin, but I come against you in the name of the Lord Almighty, the God of the armies of Israel, whom you have defied" (1 Samuel 17:45, NIV), showcasing his spiritual armor in action.

David's story vividly illustrates how faith, reliance on God's word, and righteousness (right standing with God) equip us for life's battles, aligning with the metaphorical Armor of God that

Paul describes in Ephesians 6. This narrative teaches that true strength and victory come not from physical armor or weapons but from being spiritually prepared and grounded in faith.

Recognizing the Signs of Spiritual Battles

Sometimes, we might feel worried, scared, or tempted to do things we know are wrong. These feelings can be signs of the spiritual battles we face. Just like David, we can remember to put on our Armor of God to help us stand strong and overcome these challenges with God's help.

Overcoming through the Armor of God

No matter what we face, the Armor of God is always there to protect us and give us strength. Whether we're dealing with a tough day at school, a fight with a friend, or feeling worried about how something will turn out, we can pray and remember each piece of God's Armor to help us through.

Activities and Reflections

Pictionary: Spiritual vs. Physical Battles

Play a game of Pictionary with your friends or family. In this game, you draw things related to physical battles (like knights and castles) and spiritual battles (like prayer, love, and kindness).

This will help you see the difference and remember how to fight the real battle with God's help.

Spiritual Warrior Badge of Honor

Create a special badge that represents each piece of the Armor of God. You can draw, color, and decorate your badges and wear them as a reminder that you're a strong warrior for God, ready for any battle that comes your way.

Family Discussion: Supporting Each Other in Battles

Sit down with your family and talk about times when you've faced tough challenges and how you've helped each other through them. Share how putting on the Armor of God (like being truthful, choosing what's right, and remembering God's love) helped you overcome these challenges together.

Understanding the real battle and learning how to wear the Armor of God makes you a warrior in God's kingdom! Remember, no matter what battles we face, with God's Armor, we're never fighting alone. So, let's stand strong, support each other, and face every challenge with courage and love!

Conclusion: Embracing the Full Armor

"Therefore take up the whole armor of God, that you may be able to withstand in the evil day, and having done all, to stand." Eph-esians 6:13

Dear young warriors, we've journeyed together through the incredible Armor of God, discovering each piece and its unique power. Now, as we reach the end of this adventure, let's understand how all these pieces work together to protect and empower us every single day.

The Interconnectedness of the Armor

Imagine each piece of the Armor of God like parts of a noble knight's armor. Just like a knight needs every part of their suit to be fully protected and strong, we need every piece of God's armor. The Belt of Truth keeps us rooted in honesty, the Breast-plate of Righteousness protects our hearts, the Shoes of Peace guide our steps, the Shield of Faith defends against doubts, the Helmet of Salvation keeps our minds safe, and the Sword of the Spirit, which is God's Word, gives us wisdom and strength. When we wear all these pieces together, we're fully equipped to face anything that comes our way.

Kids Being Prepared for Their Daily Spiritual Journey

Every day is an adventure filled with new challenges and opportunities. Just like getting ready for school in the morning, putting on the Armor of God prepares you for the day ahead. It's not about wearing physical armor but about remembering God's truths, choosing what's right, finding peace in His promises, trusting in His protection, knowing His love saves us, and using His word to guide us. This way, no matter what you face—whether it's a tough test, a disagreement with a friend, or feeling scared or alone—you're ready and strong because you're wearing God's special armor.

Stand Firm in Faith

Now, brave adventurers, it's your turn to stand tall and confident in your faith. Remember, you are never alone on this journey. God is always with you, offering His Armor to protect and strengthen you. When you wake up each day, think about putting on each piece of the Armor of God. You can even say a little prayer as you imagine putting on each piece, asking God to help you live out His truths, make choices that please Him, and spread kindness and peace wherever you go.

You are God's mighty warrior, equipped with an incredible Armor that makes you ready for anything. With the Armor of God, you can be a shining light of faith, hope, and love to everyone around you. So, stand firm, keep the faith, and take on each new day with courage and joy, knowing you're wearing the most powerful armor there is—the Armor of God.

Thank you for joining this adventure through the Armor of God. You're now fully equipped to face your daily challenges with strength, courage, and wisdom. Wear your armor proudly, young warriors, and go forth in the strength of God's mighty power!

Adventures in Scriptures

Other Books in the Series

If you enjoyed and found inspiration reading Exploring The Full Armor of God, you won't want to miss the other captivating volumes in our series. Each book takes a deeper look into key biblical themes and virtues, offering a treasure trove of wisdom and guidance for your spiritual journey. From "Exploring the Fruit of the Spirit" to the uplifting lessons in "Exploring the Parable Teachings of Jesus," our series is designed to nurture your soul, strengthen your faith, and light your path. Let's set out on this continuing adventure to discover more about love, grace, and the transformative power of faith. Let each page turn be a step closer to a deeper understanding and a fuller heart. Join us as we explore the riches of God's word and the endless beauty it holds for our lives.

1. Exploring the Fruit of the Spirit

2. Exploring The Full Armor of God

3. Exploring the Parable Teachings of Jesus

4. Exploring the Great Men of the Bible

5. Exploring the Great Women of the Bible

6. Exploring the Life of Jesus

We hope "Exploring the Full Armor of God" has been a source of inspiration and growth on your spiritual journey. If this book has touched your heart, illuminated your path, or brought new insights into your life, we'd be honored if you would share your experience. Please take a moment to leave a review. Your feedback not only supports our work but also guides others in their quest for spiritual enrichment. Share how "Exploring The Full Armor of God" has blessed you with a better understanding of the Armor of God that it may inspire others on this journey of faith. Leave your review today and help spread the seeds of faith and knowledge. Thank you for being a part of our community and for your invaluable contribution to this shared journey.

Biblical References Notices

NKJV

Scripture taken from the New King James Version®. Copyright © 1982 by Thomas Nelson. Used by permission. All rights reserved. All Scripture quotations

NIV

Scripture quotations marked (NIV) are taken from the Holy Bible, New International Version®, NIV®. Copyright © 1973, 1978, 1984, 2011 by Biblica, Inc.™ Used by permission of Zondervan. All rights reserved worldwide. www.zondervan.comThe "NIV" and "New International Version" are trademarks registered in the United States Patent and Trademark Office by Biblica, Inc.™

NLT

Scripture quotations marked (NLT) are taken from the Holy Bible, New Living Translation, copyright ©1996, 2004, 2015 by Tyndale House Foundation. Used by permission of Tyndale House Publishers, Carol Stream, Illinois 60188. All rights reserved.